A Cake All For Me!

by **Karen Magnuson Beil**

illustrated by **Paul Meisel**

SCHOLASTIC INC.

New York Toronto London Auckland Sydney
Mexico City New Delhi Hong Kong

Warm up the oven.
Grease up a pan.
I'll bake a big cake
fast as I can.

One, two, get out the moo.

Three, four, open and pour.

Five, six, sift and mix.

OINK
ENRICHED

PIGGY
FLOUR

PIGLET
SALT

— 2 Cups

— 1 Cup

Tbsp.

Seven, eight, chop and grate.

1 CUP

SOW
BRAND

CHOCOLATE
CHIPS

Nine, ten, eggs from the hen,

"Oh, a cake all for me, all for me!"

Eleven, twelve, take sugar from the shelf.

Thirteen, fourteen, measuring, sorting.

Fifteen, sixteen, a big bowl for mixing;

Seventeen, eighteen, the cake is baking.

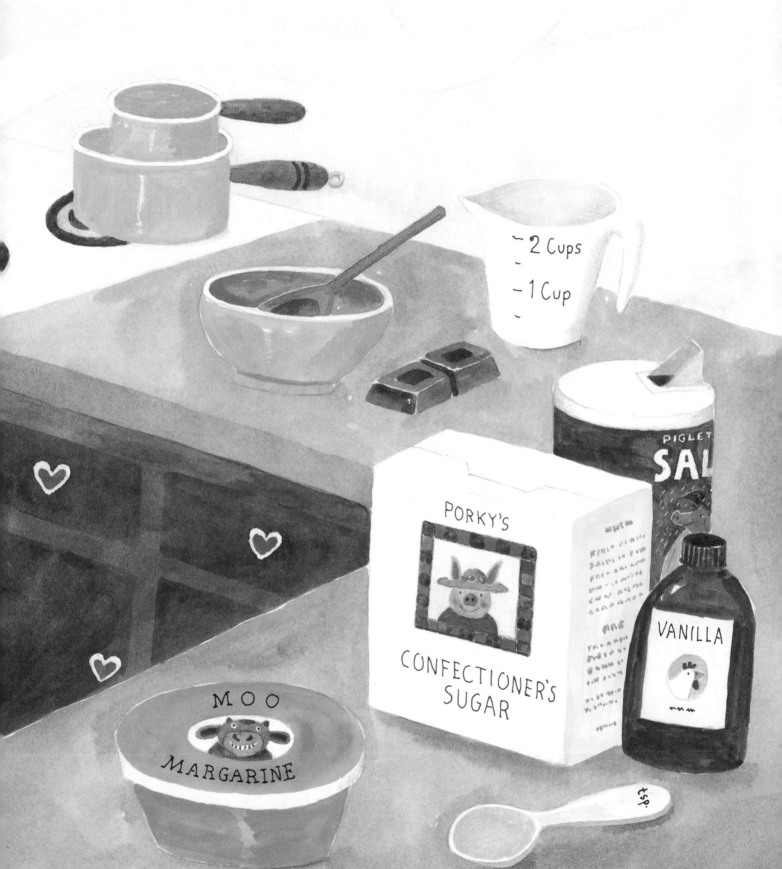

"No! A cake all for ME, all for ME!"

"I'm starving!"
"I'm hungry!"
"I'm famished!" they said.
"A cake all for us, all for us?"

"A cake all for me would be easy to slice.

But a cake shared with friends tastes mighty nice."

"A CAKE ALL FOR

US, ALL FOR US!"

Measurements

Measuring spoons come in sets that have one tablespoon,

one teaspoon,

one 1/2 teaspoon,

one 1/4 teaspoon,

and one 1/8 teaspoon.

One tablespoon equals 3 teaspoons.

One cup equals two 1/2 cups,

three 1/3 cups,

or four 1/4 cups.

Milk comes in gallons, half gallons, quarts, pints, and cups.

One gallon equals two 1/2 gallons,

4 quarts,

8 pints,

or 16 cups.

One 1/2 gallon equals 2 quarts,

4 pints,

or 8 cups.

One quart equals 2 pints,

or 4 cups.

One pint equals 2 cups.

One pound equals 16 ounces.

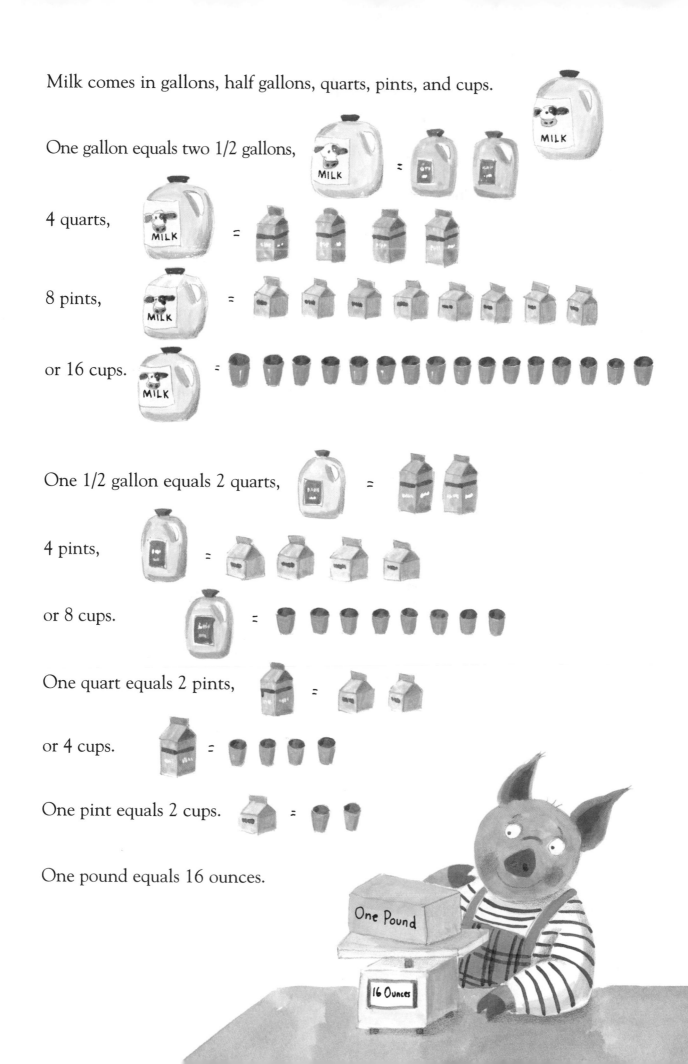

PIGGY'S POLKA-DOT CAKE
Ask an adult to help you cook!

nonstick cooking spray or margarine

3 cups plus 3 tablespoons flour

1 cup milk

1 teaspoon vanilla

3 teaspoons baking powder

1 teaspoon salt

1 apple

4 eggs

1 tablespoon of grated orange rind

2 cups of sugar

1 1/2 cups margarine (3 sticks)

1 cup chocolate chips

1. Heat the oven to 350 degrees. Wash your hands thoroughly with warm water and soap. Grease a 9" x 13" cake pan with nonstick cooking spray or margarine. Sprinkle 3 tablespoons of flour inside the pan, then tilt and gently tap the pan to coat the bottom and sides with a light dusting of flour. Shake the extra flour out onto a piece of waxed paper and put it back into the flour container.

2. Pour 1 cup of milk. Add 1 teaspoon of vanilla to the milk in the measuring cup.

3. Sift and mix together 3 cups of flour, 3 teaspoons of baking powder, and 1 teaspoon of salt.

4. Measure 1 cup of chocolate chips. Peel one apple and remove its core. Ask a grown-up to chop the apple into tiny pieces.

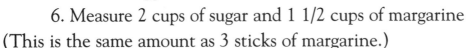

5. Crack 4 eggs into a small bowl.

6. Measure 2 cups of sugar and 1 1/2 cups of margarine (This is the same amount as 3 sticks of margarine.)

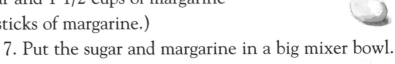

7. Put the sugar and margarine in a big mixer bowl. Beat the sugar and margarine until the mixture is creamy. Add the eggs; beat well. Add the flour and milk mixtures, alternating them a little at a time like this: flour, milk, flour, milk, flour. Beat again until it is completely mixed. Stir in the chocolate chips, the chopped apple, and the grated orange peel. Pour the mixture into the 9" x 13" pan.

8. Ask a grown-up to put the pan on a rack in the center of the oven. Bake for 40 to 45 minutes, or until a toothpick stuck in the cake comes out clean—with no gooey cake globs stuck to it. Ask a grown-up to take the cake from the oven. While the cake cools, make Piggy's Choc-o-Lot Frosting.

PIGGY'S CHOC-O-LOT FROSTING

2 ounces of unsweetened chocolate
2 teaspoons margarine
1/4 cup hot water

1/8 teaspoon salt
2 1/2 cups powdered confectioner's sugar
1 teaspoon vanilla

1. Ask a grown-up to help you melt 2 ounces of unsweetened chocolate in a double-boiler over medium heat.

2. Add 2 teaspoons of margarine to the chocolate, letting the margarine melt into the chocolate. Ask a grown-up to remove the double-boiler from the hot burner and put it on a rack to cool.

3. Add 1/4 cup of hot water and 1/8 teaspoon of salt to the chocolate.

4. Sift 2 1/2 cups of powdered confectioner's sugar into a medium-sized bowl. Then stir it into the chocolate mixture.

5. Add 1 teaspoon of vanilla to the sugar-and-chocolate mixture; stir it until it is smooth.

6. When your cake is cool, spread this frosting all over the top of it.

7. Wash and dry all the dishes, then put them where they belong.

8. This is the most important step: Eat the cake and enjoy it— with friends!

Two cups love, one laughter, a book for Dad
—K. M. B.

For my mother, who has made lots of yummy polka-dot
cookies and cakes over the years
—P. M.

With thanks to teachers who inspire—
Bette Darwin, Ed Meskutovecz, Kathy Oboyski-Butler,
Karen Shields, and Nancy von Daacke.

ISBN 0-439-08724-4

12 11 10 9 8 7 6 5 4 3 2 1   9/9 0 1 2 3 4/0

Printed in the U.S.A.   14

First Scholastic printing, November 1999

A Cake All For Me!

by **Karen Magnuson Beil**

illustrated by **Paul Meisel**

SCHOLASTIC